Contents

Acknowledgements	3
The Cheshire Hoards	4
The Malpas Hoard	
The discovery	7
The content of the hoard	8
Caratacus	11
The Knutsford Hoard	
The discovery	12
The content of the hoard	13
Commodus's war in northern Britain	21
Other Trumpet Brooches from north west England	22
The Peover Hoard	24
Roman Coinage	26
Metallurgy of coins	27
How to Read a Roman coin	29
The Romano-British North West	31
Chester and the Military Presence	32
Settlements	34
Industry and Trade	37
Edge of Empire	38
Conclusions	39
Timeline	40
Places to Visit	42
Further Reading	44

Acknowledgements

The discovery, reporting, research, acquisition and display of the Cheshire Hoards has involved many people working co-operatively.

The finders reported the hoards to the Portable Antiquities Scheme (PAS) Finds Liaison Officer, Vanessa Oakden. The Knutsford Hoard was excavated by members of the Museum of Liverpool archaeology team, led by Rob Philpott, alongside Alan Bates the finder. The landowner at Knutsford enabled access for detailed archaeological investigation, and recording of findspots of this dispersed hoard.

At the British Museum, the Treasure team co-ordinated work on the hoards. Sam Moorhead and colleagues identified the coins. Pippa Pearce undertook important conservation work, cleaning the objects to enable full identification and valuation prior to acquisition. Ben Jones undertook additional work cataloguing the Knutsford Hoard following cleaning of the finds.

The staff at Congleton Museum, Ian Doughty and Jean Westbrook, worked closely with the Museum of Liverpool team to deliver the project and ensure that the collections will be used and enjoyed by thousands of museum visitors in the north west.

The Cheshire Hoards project has involved members of the Mersey and Dee Young Archaeologists' Club (YAC) working with the finds, and learning about them to create some of the interpretation. Many thanks to the members and leaders of YAC and to Handstand Productions, Roman Tours Chester, Travellers Through Time and Little Lamb Tales, who provided workshops for YAC.

This project would not have been possible without the funding from the Heritage Lottery Fund, to whom we are very grateful.

The Cheshire Hoards

The discovery of two hoards of Roman coins and jewellery in 2012 and 2014 has provided an opportunity to explore the first and second centuries AD and consider the means by which wealth may have accumulated, the reasons for the deposition of objects, and the question of non-retrieval of the items.

We don't know exactly who buried either of the hoards, but they must have been fairly wealthy individuals who had amassed these coins and jewellery items. They would have been buried for safekeeping, possibly at a time of turmoil.

The ultimate mystery of any hoard is why the owner never returned to collect it, and we can never be certain of the reason. We do, however, know that both the Malpas and Knutsford Hoards were buried at times of political instability and uncertainty.

This book explores the stories of the Malpas and Knutsford Hoards and other finds from the region.

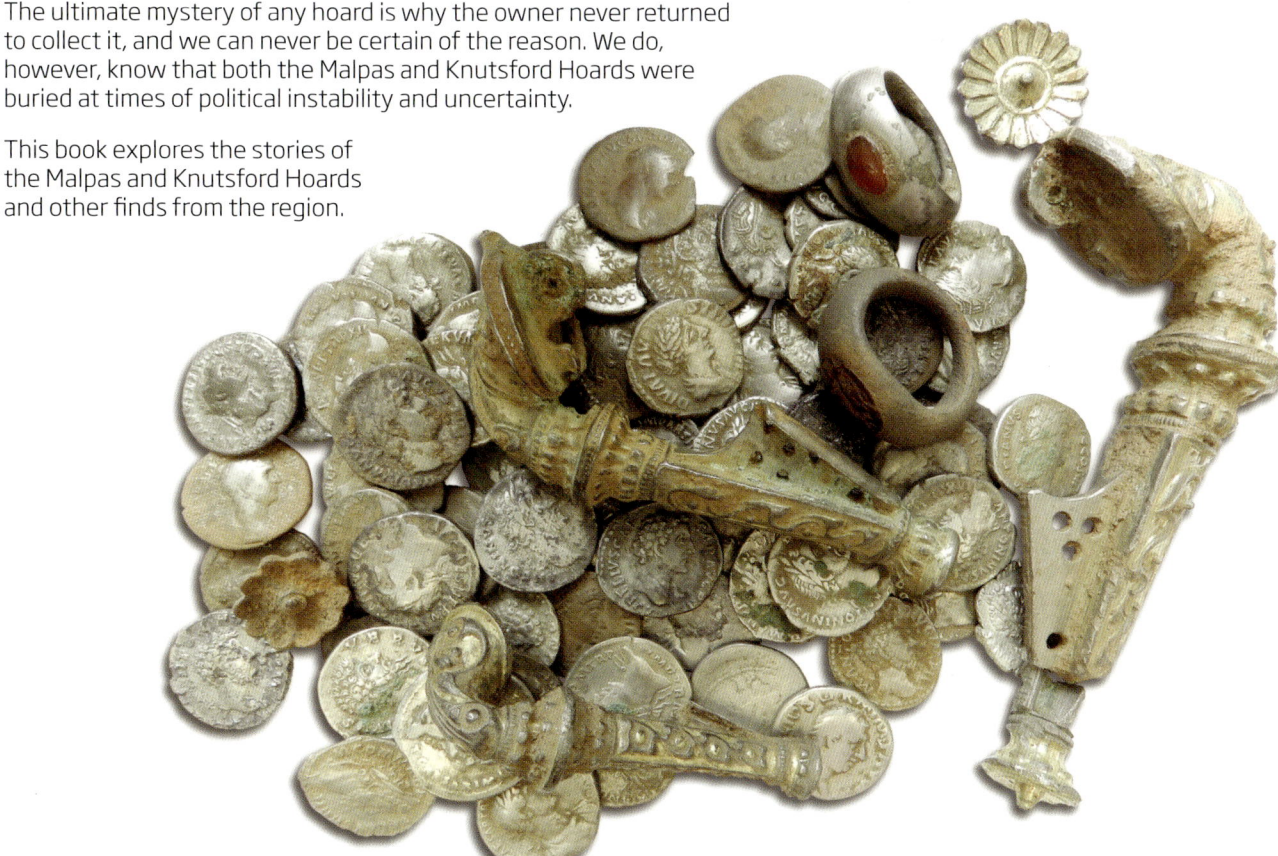

The 1st and 2nd century phase of Roman occupation and the initial period of contact between the Roman army and the Britons of the north west remains the subject of considerable debate and research. The Romans were in Britain for a long time, the equivalent of the period from the English Civil War to the modern day, and there were considerable changes in leadership structures, lifestyles, economies and fashions through this period.

At the time when the south and east of Britain were Romanised, the north and west remained less so throughout the Roman period. There was a military presence at Chester, a developing network of roads, and an active trading port at Meols, Wirral. However, much of the rural agriculturally-based settlement in the north west retained similarities to Iron Age lifestyles.

A reconstructed Iron Age farm at Castell Henllys, Pembrokeshire, represents what life would have been like in early Roman north west England.

The Malpas Hoard

The Discovery

The Malpas hoard was discovered during a metal detecting rally near the parish of Malpas in January 2014. Rallies bring metal-detectorists together for a day to detect together over several fields. The finds were then taken to the Grosvenor Museum, Chester, where they were handed in to the PAS Finds Liaison Officer Vanessa Oakden and were reported to the coroner and entered into the Treasure process.

The Malpas Hoard
Treasure case: 2014T89

Portable Antiquities Scheme reference number: LVPL-DFD9E1

Museum of Liverpool accession number: MOL.2015.51

The areas controlled by the major Iron Age tribes of Britain.

Content of the Hoard

The Malpas Hoard is a group of 35 coins which were struck between 134BC and around AD50. There are seven Iron Age British coins made between AD20 and AD50. The Roman coins are very early examples, struck before the conquest of Britain, and of the type that would have been in circulation when Roman soldiers arrived in Britain in AD43. The latest coin, a denarius of Tiberius (AD14-37) isn't very worn, which suggests that the hoard would have been buried within about ten years of the Roman conquest.

The seven Iron Age coins, known as staters, are among over 30,000 Iron Age coins which have been found in Britain. There are three examples of the type common in the western area, especially Gloucestershire, marked 'EISV', and four examples of those from the east, Lincolnshire and Leicestershire, marked 'VEP CORF'. This mixture of coins from the two areas within one hoard is very unusual.

'EISV' western coins are usually associated with the Dobunni tribe, and 'VEP CORF' eastern coins with the Corieltauvi tribe.

The Roman coins

Accession Number	Moneyer/Issuer	Date	Weight (g)
MOL.2015.51.8	Ti. Minucius C.f. Augurinus	134 BC	3.46
MOL.2015.51.9	Mn. Aemilius Lepidus	114/113 BC	3.41
MOL.2015.51.10	L. Flaminius Chilo	109-108 BC	3.45
MOL.2015.51.11	L. Julius	101 BC	3.49
MOL.2015.51.12	D. Silanus L. f.	91 BC	3.52
MOL.2015.51.13	Q. Titius	90 BC	2.86
MOL.2015.51.14	Probably L. Rutilius Flaccus	77 BC	2.88
MOL.2015.51.15	M. Plaetorius M.f. Cestianus.	67 BC	3.11
MOL.2015.51.16	L RosciusFabatus (denarius serratus)	64 BC	3.39
MOL.2015.51.17	L. Aemilius Lepidus Paullus	62 BC	3.44
MOL.2015.51.18	M. AemiliusScaurus and P. Hypsaeus	58 BC	3.53
MOL.2015.51.19	A. Plautius	55BC	3.46
MOL.2015.51.20	Mn. Acilius Gabrio	49 BC	3.51
MOL.2015.51.21	Mn. Acilius Gabrio	49 BC	3.61
MOL.2015.51.22	C. Vibius C.f. C.n. Pansa	48 BC	3.27
MOL.2015.51.23	Julius Caesar	44 BC	1.01
MOL.2015.51.24	Octavian	42 BC	3.39
MOL.2015.51.25	Brutus	43/42 BC	3.36
MOL.2015.51.26	Mark Antony	31 BC	3.20
MOL.2015.51.27	Uncertain Republican denarius	c. 120-70 BC	3.21

Accession Number	Issuer	Obverse	Reverse	W (g)
MOL.2015.51.28	Augustus	AVGVSTVS DIVI F	IMP.X (bull butting right)	3.46
MOL.2015.51.29	Augustus	CAESAR AVGVSTVS DIVI F PATER PATRIAE	TI CAESA[R AVG F] T POT XV (Tiberius in triumphal quadriga right)	3.53
MOL.2015.51.30	Tiberius	TI CAESAR DIVI AVG F AVGVSTVS	PONTIF MAXIM (Pax seated right)	3.49
MOL.2015.51.31	Tiberius	TI CAESAR DIVI AVG F AVGVSTVS	PONTIF MAXIM (Pax seated right)	3.40
MOL.2015.51.32	Tiberius	TI CAESAR DIVI AVG F AVGVSTVS	PONTIF MAXIM (Pax seated right)	3.53
MOL.2015.51.33	Tiberius	TI CAESAR DIVI AVG F AVGVSTVS	PONTIF MAXIM (Pax seated right)	3.51
MOL.2015.51.34	Tiberius	TI CAESAR DIVI AVG F AVGVSTVS	PONTIF MAXIM (Pax seated right)	3.04
MOL.2015.51.35	Tiberius	TI CAESAR DIVI AVG F AVGVSTVS	PONTIF MAXIM (Pax seated right)	3.04

Caratacus

The burial of the Malpas hoard around the late AD40s or 50s has led Sam Moorhead of the British Museum to suggest that it might be associated with the defeat and capture of Caratacus, leader of the Catuvellauni. After their arrival in AD43, the Roman army targeted the Catuvellauni settlement of Colchester, and the tribe held out against the army for over ten years. However, in AD51, Caratacus was finally defeated, and fled to northern England, an area under the control of Queen Cartimandua of the Brigantes. Cartimandua handed Caratacus over to the Romans but the historian Tacitus records that he escaped punishment by death by making a powerful speech to Emperor Claudius. It's possible the coins were part of the wealth Caratacus or his comrades amassed, and buried for the future, but were unable to recover after he was captured and taken to Rome.

The Knutsford Hoard

The Discovery

The Knutsford Hoard was found in 2012 by Alan Bates. When Alan had uncovered a handful of coins and had located several areas where his metal detector was recording strong signals, he immediately called the PAS Finds Liaison Officer Vanessa Oakden, and reported the find. A team of archaeologists from the Museum of Liverpool and Cheshire Archaeological Advisory Service, led by Rob Philpott, worked with Alan to recover and record the hoard, which had been partially ploughed-out and was spread across the field.

Finder, Alan Bates and Finds Liaison Officer, Vanessa Oakden.

Treasure case: 2012T406

Portable Antiquities Scheme reference number: LVPL-B44185

Museum of Liverpool accession number: MOL.2015.90

Content of the Hoard

The Knutsford Hoard consists of 103 coins, three brooches, and two finger rings. It's likely that Roman 'Wilderspool Oxidised Ware' pottery found associated with these finds was once a container for them, but recent ploughing unwittingly broke the pot and spread the finds across the field.

The coins range in date from 32BC to the end of the second century. 101 are silver denarii, and two are copper alloy sestertii.

Archaeologists and metal-detectorist, Alan Bates, excavated the site together.

The coins

Issuer	Date/period	Number of denarii
Mark Antony	coins dated 32-31BC	2
Galba	AD 69	1
Vitellius	AD 69	2
Vespasian	AD 69-79	8
Titus under Vespasian	AD 69-79	1
Titus	AD 79-81	1
Domitian under Titus	AD 79-81	2
Domitian	AD 81-96	3
Nerva	AD 96-98	2
Trajan	AD 98-117	11
Uncertain Hadrian or Trajan	AD 98-138	2
Hadrian	AD 117-38	13 + 1 sestertius
Sabina under Hadrian	AD 128-138 or posthumously 138 onwards	1
Antoninus Pius	AD 138-61	13 + 1 sestertius
Faustina I under Antoninus Pius	AD139-141	1
Diva Faustina I under Antoninus Pius	AD 140 onwards	5
Marcus Aurelius as Caesar under Antoninus Pius	AD 140-161	4
Marcus Aurelius	AD 161-180	6
Lucius Verus under Marcus Aurelius	AD 161-180	1
Marcus Aurelius in honour of Divys Verus	AD 169	1
Lucilla under Marcus Aurelius	AD 161-169	2
Faustina II under Marcus Aurelius	AD 161-175	5

Issuer	Date/period	Number of denarii
Diva Faustina II under Marcus Aurelius	AD 176-180	1
Commodus as Caesar under Marcus Aurelius	AD 172-176	1
Commodus	AD 180-92	9
Crispina under Commodus	AD 180-92	1
Ancient Forgery		1
Probable denarius		1
	Total	**101 + 2 sestertii**

The earliest coin is a Roman Republican coin of Mark Antony. These coins are known to have circulated for a long period in Britain, and certainly during the second century AD. The range of coins and overall composition of the group is typical for a hoard deposited towards the end of the second century AD. Whilst hoards containing both silver denarii and copper alloy sestertii are less common than those containing coins of one metal, there are others recorded from this period and there is no doubt that the two sestertii belong to the hoard. It's possible that the larger sestertii were used as stoppers for the ceramic container in which the valuable denarii were stored. The date of the latest coins in the group is consistent with the date of the jewellery items and indicates a probable burial in the AD180s or 190s.

The Brooches

The three brooches of the Knutsford Hoard are large examples of 'trumpet' brooches, so named after their open circular ends. They are made from silver and surfaced with gold. The gilding, of a type called parcel-gilding, fills recesses and allows the silver to show on raised areas, creating a two-colour effect. The earliest trumpet brooches were made in the AD70s and the type is common throughout the second century AD. Trumpet brooches are found in Roman Britain, but not elsewhere in the Empire, a British take on a Roman style of brooch. The decoration on these examples derives from Iron Age swirling La Tène style patterns, which suggest the expression of a local British identity through these objects.

The brooches would have been made in a mould. The incredible detail in the decoration of these items came from the detailed work in making the mould. Some brooches have mould lines visible on them, showing they were made in a two-part reusable mould. Further decoration was added after moulding, including the perforation of the catchplate at the rear of the brooch, a detail not visible when the item is worn.

These trumpet brooches would have had 'headloops', a metal loop attachment on the round 'trumpet' end, which would probably have been used for attaching a chain if brooches were worn in pairs. The examples from Knutsford were found associated with rosettes, which would have adorned the headloops as decoration.

The Rings

The two finger rings in of the Knutsford Hoard are cast silver with inlaid carnelian stone intaglios. One of the intaglios is decorated with an incised design, which is a depiction of a winged figure, probably Victory. The other ring has a plain intaglio but the shape of it suggests that it may have been filed down in antiquity, possibly reflecting a change in fashion or shifting interests in different deities.

While both the rings are of metal alloys containing silver they have very different surfaces suggesting that the silver alloys from which they are made may be of different qualities.

Who wore such jewellery?

Establishing who might have worn brooches like these is difficult: they are large examples, which possibly suggests they were for men; but they have headloops for chains, which are a feature more often associated with women's jewellery. While brooches were originally developed to fasten clothing, the types of clothes more commonly worn in Britain didn't require them, so the brooches may just have been for decoration, or for fastening over-garments. In the past trumpet brooches like these have been thought to be associated with the military, and many examples have been found on military sites, but these finds are from well outside a military context, either indicating a civilian use or placing military personnel in an unusual location.

The rings are very small, which might suggest they were for a female hand, but they could have been worn on the fifth finger or on the lower knuckle of a man's hand. Intaglios could be worn for decoration only or have had a functional purpose in sealing letters and documents. This would have been carried out more commonly by men, but also by women.

The wearing of different types of jewellery would have varied widely across the vast Roman Empire. Earrings were a solely female jewellery item among Romans, but Roman historian Pliny writes about ear-rings that 'in the East, indeed, it is considered becoming even for men to wear gold in that place [the ear lobe]' describing common practice among men in Syria and the middle east.

A Romano-British woman wearing a pair of trumpet brooches.
Illustrated by Chris Rodenhurst

The ceramics

Over 40 fragments of pottery were discovered in the vicinity of the coins of the Knutsford Hoard. It is assumed that these are the broken remains of a pot which has been damaged by ploughing. The pottery is a locally made type of Roman age, known as Wilderspool Oxidised ware. It's impossible now to know the original shape of the vessel.

Romano-British man burying his wealth for safekeeping.
Illustrated by Chris Rodenhurst

Commodus's War in Northern Britain

The Knutsford Hoard was buried at the close of the second century AD. This was a period of war in northern Britain, "[Commodus (AD180-193)] fought with barbarians beyond Dacia (modern Romania) ... but the greatest war was in Britain. The people of the island, having crossed the wall which divides them from the legions, did a great deal of damage and killed a certain general and the soldiers with him" (Dio 72.8.1-2).

Little is known about this war, but archaeological finds from Hadrian's Wall area suggest there may have been a phase of destruction around this period at Halton Chesters, Rudchester and Corbridge at Hadrian's Wall.

The 'trumpet' brooches of the type found in the Knutsford Hoard are sometimes associated with the military, so it's possible the person who buried them may have been a senior soldier in the army preparing for battle and fearing the worst.

Other Trumpet Brooches from north west England

Trumpet Brooch from Church Minshull, Cheshire

Portable Antiquities Scheme reference number: IARCH-107D14/IARCH-BABBC3

In 2004 the Church Minshull Hoard was discovered containing 58 denarii, beginning with Mark Antony and ending with Faustina Junior. It was perhaps deposited around AD176, but an earlier date is possible. It also contained two silver-gilt trumpet brooches. One of the brooches was estimated at between 80 and 90mm long but it was deliberately broken and is incomplete. The head decoration is very similar to the Knutsford example.

Trumpet Brooch from Tarvin, Cheshire

Portable Antiquities Scheme reference number: LVPL534

This Copper alloy trumpet brooch has ornate moulded decoration and traces of tinning/silvering. There are remnants of a corroded iron spring attached.

Trumpet Brooch from Kendal, Cumbria

Portable Antiquities Scheme reference number: LVPL55

This ornately decorated copper alloy trumpet brooch is an unusually complete example. It has a surviving attached headloop with a decorative rosette with a small central boss surrounded by fifteen 'petals'. The pin is missing.

Trumpet Brooch from Malpas, Cheshire

Portable Antiquities Scheme reference number: LVPL-4F4C76

This example is a highly decorated cast copper alloy trumpet brooch. Like one of the Knutsford examples, the catchplate has been perforated three times for decoration.

Pair of Trumpet Brooches and chain from Chorley, Lancashire

British Museum accession number 1850,1106.2

Very few trumpet brooches survive in such completeness as this pair found in Chorley in the Victorian period. Such finds provide strong evidence about the original form and use of such jewellery items.

© British Museum

The Peover Hoard

A hoard of over 7,000 copper alloy 'radiate' coins was discovered in 2015 near Peover in Cheshire, many still inside a large ceramic jar, others distributed following plough damage to the top of the vessel. The coins, all dating to the third century AD, were each of low value, and would have been very common in circulation as small change. The vast quantity of coins amassed must have represented considerable savings for the person or people who buried them.

The finders of the hoard contacted Vanessa Oakden, PAS Finds Liaison Officer, and a team of archaeologists from the Museum of Liverpool excavated the finds with the metal-detectorists, plotting and recording the scatter of coins across the field. The pot containing the vast majority of the coins was lifted in a soil block and transported to the British Museum for controlled excavation and detailed analysis in the conservation laboratory.

The Peover Hoard under excavation.

Right: The Peover Hoard under analysis at the British Museum.   © British Museum

Treasure case: 2015T46

Portable Antiquities Scheme reference number: LVPL-E332C6

Roman Coinage

Coinage had been circulating in Britain for some time before the Roman invasion, but as Britain was incorporated into the Roman Empire the internationally-recognised state-backed currency became a primary means of making transactions.

Several different denominations of coin circulated:

Aureus (gold)	= 25 Denarii
Denarius (silver)	= 2 Quinarii
Quinarius (silver)	= 2 Sestertii
Sestertius	= 2 Dupondii
Dupondius	= 2 Asses
As (copper)	= 2 Semiasses
Semis (copper)	= 2 Quadrantes

Roman legionary soldiers' pay in 2nd century AD would have been around 300 denarii a year. These payments alone represent a very large number of coins present and circulating in Britain, some of which were hoarded, while others have been recovered archaeologically as chance losses.

Coins in Britain would have been struck in many different places, commonly in Rome or Gaul (France) or, by the later 3rd century AD in London.

Roman silver alloy denarii.

Metallurgy of Coins

While there was a well-established system of coinage in the Roman Empire, the value of coins and the composition of metals used to make them changed over time as the economy shifted. In the second century AD there was inflation across the Roman Empire, and increasing amounts of copper were added to the silver to make coins. This 'debasement' meant that by the end of the second century a 'silver' denarius would contain only about 50% silver. Thus, the coins of the earlier Malpas Hoard would have held more value when they were in use than those of the Knutsford Hoard, which dates some 150 years later.

The adding of more copper to silver coins to 'debase' them increased, and by the end of the third century AD there was only around 5% silver in coinage. This parallels the 20th century shift from the use of silver in coins like the pre-decimal sixpence, to the use of cupro-nickel for 5, 10, 20 and 50p coins, and from 2012 5p and 10p cupro-nickel coins were replaced with nickel-plated steel coins.

Modern coins made from metal alloys.

How to read a Roman coin

The Bust

The front or 'obverse' of a Roman coin usually depicts the ruler, emperor or empress. They are shown as a bust, a side view of their head, as is the Queen on our coins today.

The bust of the issuer of a coin is sometimes the quickest and easiest way to identify the broad date of a coin. Many of the busts are realistic depictions of the issuer.

Personification

The back or 'reverse' of a coin often has a personification on it – these are Gods, virtues represented in human form, such as 'peace', or military or religious symbols.

Mars – God of War

Salus – Goddess of safety and wellbeing

Jupiter – King of the Roman Gods, shown holding thunderbolt

Venus – Goddess of love and beauty, shown holding Victory and resting left hand on shield

Aequitas – Goddess of fairness

Providentia – personification of making provision for the future, shown holding cornucopia

Hilaritas – personification of cheefulness, shown arranging her hair!

The Legend

The lettering surrounding the bust contains a lot of information about the coin and its issuer. The lettering will name the emperor and give his titles and some of his attributes, such as:

IMP - Imperator - Emperor of the Roman Empire, and leader of the army

CAES or CAESAR - Caesar - a title taken by emperors demonstrating their descent (whether directly by blood or not) from Julius Caesar

AVG - Augustus - a title taken by emperors meaning 'majestic' or 'venerable'

AVGVSTA - female of Augustus

COS - CONSUL - The consuls were the chief magistrates of the Roman government. This title is often followed by a numeral which indicates the number of times the Emperor had held this position

'PF' or PIUS - Pius Felix - meaning dutiful and wise

S C - Senatus Consulto - 'by decree of the senate' - the Emperor controlled gold and silver coins, and copper alloy coins were controlled by the senate

SPQR - Senatus Populus que Romanus - of the Senate and People of Rome

Animals

Several reverses of these coins portray animals which often have meaning.

Eagle – symbol associated with the Roman army

Peacock – associated with or a representation of Goddess Juno, protector of the state

Salus and the snake – the Goddess of safety and well-being, Salus, is seen feeding a snake, that of her father Aesculapius, God of healing and medicine

Camel - reflecting the extents of the Roman Empire from north Africa to northern Europe

Knutsford Hoard coins showing an ibis or stork and Salus and the snake.

Malpas Hoard coins showing a bull, eagle and horses.

The Romano-British North West

The Knutsford and Malpas Hoards are part of a growing body of evidence about the Romano-British North West. Finds recorded through the Portable Antiquities Scheme enable us to see patterns of activity through chance losses and cases of deliberate burial of objects. Excavations have started to reveal evidence about lifestyles and the settlements in which people lived.

When the Romans arrived in the north west, local tribes reacted to them in different ways: the Cornovii were defeated in battle by the Roman army at Wrekin hillfort, the Deceangli surrendered to the Roman army, and the Brigantes agreed allegiance to Rome. Despite the Roman administration, many aspects of the lifestyles of people in the region were not heavily influenced by the Roman presence.

Some elements of the material culture which survive from the Roman period demonstrate clear influence of the Empire and trade. Even small farmsteads have continental pottery types represented, while in other spheres lifestyles retain much Iron Age character: people are living in roundhouses and farming their immediate landscape.

Roundhouses at Castell Henllys.

Chester and the Military Presence

The Roman military centre at Chester was founded in the AD70s, and around a decade later became home to the 20th Legion of the Roman army. The legion had been selected as one of the four to participate in Emperor Claudius's conquest of Britain, and remained here until the fourth century.

The Roman centre of Chester was a substantial settlement. The military buildings would have been laid out on a grid plan like many forts, with a central headquarters building, barrack blocks, baths, and storage buildings such as granaries, surrounded by a protective wall. Outside the wall would have been a vicus, an associated civilian settlement, which would have supplied the soldiers with much of their food, and other produce. Famously Chester had a large amphitheatre outside the fort, capable of

seating around 8,000 people. This would have been used for a variety of events, and probably entertained both the soldiers and the civilian population.

Chester was connected to a road network, established to enable the movement of military personnel and equipment, but doubtless also heavily used by civilians. Other places such as the fort at Manchester or the town at Wilderspool near Warrington were important settlements in the Roman period. However, human habitation would have had a fairly minimal impact on the landscape, which was described by Roman writer Tacitus as "a landscape of forests and estuaries". Iron Age clearance of woodland would have continued in the Romano-British period to provide additional land for farming.

Settlements

Away from Chester the north west was not heavily Romanised, and settlements were small farmsteads, often surrounded by deep ditches to keep large animals out. Aerial photographs have been used to identify Roman settlements, and there's evidence of a network of separate farms, especially in the areas of the landscape well suited to farming, and away from mosslands and sandy coasts.

A Romano-British farmer's life would have revolved around seasonal sowing and reaping of harvests. Crops included barley, spelt wheat and oats. People would also have kept animals for milk, wool and eggs, and to be slaughtered for meat, leather and bone.

People continued to live in roundhouses and their clothing would probably have been broadly recognisable to their Iron Age ancestors. However, their economy was monetised, and some of their material culture such as jewellery showed local interpretations of Roman styles.

The presence of hoards like Knutsford and Malpas, and the rich Romano-British style jewellery tell of wealth in the region, and links between the native Britons and the Roman army. Excavations at rural farmsteads such as Irby in Wirral, Birch Heath near Tarporley, and Halewood in Knowsley have provided evidence of imported pottery being used by Britons.

Industry and Trade

The coming of the Roman army would have brought large new markets for some products of the North West. This could have been a decisive economic boost for some individuals or groups. Some local settlements directly provided for the Roman army, making goods which they used to build their forts, or in their daily lives, or supplying food. For example, the people who controlled the salt extraction in the Cheshire plains held a resource which would have been vital to the preservation of meats for feeding the army. It's possible that the wealth seen in the Cheshire Hoards was, in part, gathered by powerful and entrepreneurial individuals from such trade.

Expert in Roman coinage Professor David Shotter observes that although the North West is often considered an area where Romanisation did not really take hold, the hoards from the region indicate that there was considerable wealth to be found in town and country. Those burying such hoards were the kind of people who took responsibility for local leadership and administration amongst the local tribes.

The coastal port of Meols, north Wirral, has provided extensive evidence for trade. It was situated at the mouths of two significant river estuaries, the Dee and the Mersey, and so would have had good access to the heartland of north west England. This would have included links to Cheshire salt and to the mineral resources of north Wales.

A tile produced at a Romano-British settlement at Tarbock, Knowsley for the legionary fortress at Chester.
Museum of Liverpool: 1997.78.431

Edge of Empire

Britain was at the edge of the Roman Empire from the conquest in AD43 to the end of Roman administration in AD410. Lifestyles in the south and east were transformed, but the north and west were less altered by Romanisation. However, the presence of the Roman army would have been apparent. The legionary fortress at Chester and auxiliary forts at Manchester, Northwich and Whitchurch were linked by a network of roads.

Further to the north, two different structures marked the limit of Roman control at different times: construction of Hadrian's Wall started around the AD120s, and was replaced by the more northerly Antonine Wall around AD142. However, the area of Roman control contracted back to Hadrian's Wall by around the AD160s, and gradually more of the wall and forts were built in stone.

'Roman' England and Wales probably had considerable contact with other non-Roman areas of the British Isles: Hadrian's Wall is thought to have been a relatively permeable frontier, where access was controlled but not impossible. There are gateways at the forts and milecastles which would have made it possible to pass through the defended wall if permitted to do so. There is also evidence that there was trade with Ireland, which was never invaded, but where Roman-style objects are sometimes found.

Conclusions

The Malpas Hoard consists of an unusual group of coins with sources in different areas of England. The means by which these were brought together, and the reasons for their burial and non-retrieval may link directly to political uncertainty following the Roman invasion.

The burial of the Knutsford Hoard around the AD180s-190s is shortly after the peak in hoard deposition in the second century AD in the North West, again indicating a time of political and military uncertainty. The identity of the person or people depositing the hoard is impossible to determine with any certainty. However, it might be speculated that this is the private wealth of a local landowner; the amassed wealth of a retired solider; the earnings of a soldier on service; or the joint wealth of a group of individuals. Whoever buried the items, they were looking to store their belongings for safekeeping, and then were unable to return to collect them. The mysteries of hoards remain, but the objects can provide much information about the period.

Timeline

83 BC - 30 BC — Life of Mark Antony, issuer of the earliest coins present in the Malpas and Knutsford Hoards

AD 43 — Conquest of Britain under Emperor Claudius. Aulus Palutius leads the army and becomes first Roman governor of Britain

AD 51 — Defeat and capture of Caratacus, leader of the Catuvallani

AD 77-84 — Gnaeus Julius Agricola appointed governor of Britain, he conquers Wales and leads military campaigns in the north, including Caledonia (Scotland)

55 BC — Julius Caesar makes first unsuccessful attempt to extend the Roman Empire into Britain

AD 40s/50s — Burial of Malpas Hoard

AD 60s — Legionary fortress at Chester established, and XX (20th) legion based there

AD 68-71 — Emperor Vespasian appoints Marcus Vettius Bolanus as governor. The lands of the Brigantes tribes (centred around Yorkshire) are adopted into the Roman Empire after an internal feud

AD 85-90s — Roman settlement established at Wilderspool, Warrington

Construction of Hadrian's Wall begins. Marking the northern edge of the Roman empire, this stone wall would have been a defendable line in case of attack, but the Romans would have allowed controlled movement of people through gates in the forts and milecastles.

AD120s

Introduction of new denomination 'radiate'

AD215

End of Roman administration in Britain. Fighting against the Visigoths under King Alaric took a toll on the Roman Army and the Empire was weakened. Emperor Honorius instructs Britain to look after her own defences.

AD410

AD180s

Commodus's wars in northern Britain brought a period of instability and Roman soldiers in Britain rebelled against the prefect Perennis. Emperor Commodus gave the soldiers permission to put Perennis to death. Pertinax becomes governor of Britain.

Ad180s/190s

Burial of Knutsford Hoard

AD270s

Burial of Peover Hoard

Places to Visit

Bremetennacum

This cavalry fort sits in the middle of the modern-day village of Ribchester. Although only small parts of the fort have been excavated, there have been some fantastic finds uncovered over the centuries, including the Ribchester Hoard.

Ribchester Roman Museum, near Preston, PR3 3XS

Castlefield, Manchester

The Roman fort of Mamucium or Mancunium, established around AD79, was sited near a crossing place on the River Medlock. The fort was sited on a sandstone bluff near the confluence of the Rivers Medlock and Irwell in a naturally defensible position. A reconstructed part of the fort stands on the site and is open to the public.

Castlefield, Manchester, M3 4LZ

Chester Amphitheatre

The largest Roman amphitheatre in Britain, used for entertainment and military training by the 20th Legion, based at the fortress of Deva (Chester). Excavations by English Heritage and Chester City Council in 2004-5 revealed two successive stone-built amphitheatres with wooden seating.

Little St John Street, Chester, CH1 2BN

Congleton Museum

Congleton Museum's collections span over 4,000 years, and displays explore this long history in the region. Exhibits include a beautiful Roman ring found at Sandbach.

Market Square, Congleton, CW12 1ET

Grosvenor Museum, Chester

The Grosvenor Museum has rich collections of Roman finds from the numerous excavations which have taken place in and around Chester. Displays include a unique collection of Roman tombstones.

27, Grosvenor Street, Chester, CH1 2DD

Manchester Museum

Manchester's name derives from Mancunium, the name of the Roman fort established there, and the museum explores the city's early history including the display of Roman finds excavated in the city. Also on display at Manchester is a Roman soldier's bronze diploma, his demob certificate, dated 27 February 158AD, found on the beach at Ravenglass in Cumbria.

The University of Manchester, Oxford Road, Manchester M13 9PL

Museum of Liverpool

The Museum of Liverpool's Timeline displays finds from local excavations, including from Romano-British farmsteads in Merseyside. A replica skull and reconstruction of the face of 'Leasowe Man' from the Wirral, enable visitors to see the likeness of a Romano-British person.

Pier Head, Liverpool Waterfront, L3 1DG

Wroxeter

Viriconium (Wroxeter) was the fourth largest city in Roman Britain. Within the extensive remains, a bathhouse and a reconstructed town house can be seen. Objects from excavations on display in the Museum on the site reveal the daily lives of the people who lived there.

Wroxeter, near Shrewsbury, SY5 6PH

Further Reading

Abdy, R., Williams, J. H. C. and Hill, J. D. 2004. 'Church Minshull, Cheshire' in *Treasure Annual Report* 2004. pages 174-5.

Boon, G. C. and Savory, H. N. 1975. 'A Silver Trumpet-Brooch with relief decoration, parcel-gilt, from Carmarthen, and a note on the development of the type'. *Antiquaries Journal 55,* pages 41-61.

Breeze, D.J. and Dobson, B. 1976. *Hadrian's Wall.* Allen Lane. London.

Butcher, Kevin and Ponting, Matthew. 2014. *The Metallurgy of Roman Silver Coinage: from the Reforms of Nero to the Reform of Trajan.* Cambridge University Press. Cambridge.

Cottam, E., de Jersey, P., Rudd, C., and Sills, J. 2010. *Ancient British Coinage.* Chris Rudd. Aylsham.

Crawford, M. H.1975. *Roman Republican Coinage.* Cambridge University Press. Cambridge.

de la Bédoyère, G. 2013. Roman Britain: *A New History.* Thames and Hudson. London.

Mackreth, D. F. 2011. *Brooches in Late Iron Age and Roman Britain.* Oxbow Books. Oxford.

Mattingly, H. and Sydenham, E.A. 1926. *Roman Imperial Coinage Volume II: Vespasian to Hadrian.* Spink. London.

Mattingly, H. and Sydenham, E.A. 1930. *Roman Imperial Coinage Volume III: Antoninus Pius to Commodus.* Spink. London.

Oakden, V. 2015. *50 Finds From Cheshire.* Amberly. Stroud.

Shotter, D. C. A. 2011. *Roman Coins from North-West England: The Third Supplement.* Centre for North-West Regional Studies, Lancaster University. Lancaster.

Southern, P. 2013. *Roman Britain.* Amberly.Stroud.

Tomber, R. and Dore, J. 1998.*The National Roman Fabric Reference Collection* MoLAS.English Heritage.British Museum.

Van Arsdell, R.D. 1989. *Celtic Coinage of Britain.* Spink. London.